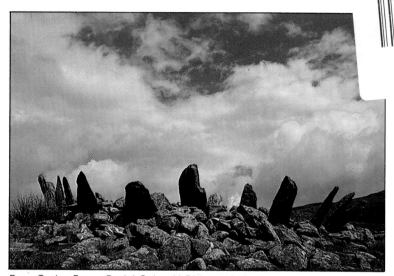

Bryn Cader Faner Burial Cairn, Y Rhinog, Ardudwy

COVER PHOTOGRAPH: Tryfan from across Cwm Idwal

First impression: 1993
Second impression: 1999
© Anthony Griffiths & Y Lolfa Cyf., 1993

Author photograph: Majorie Griffiths

ISBN: 0 86243 276 6

Published and printed in Wales by
Y Lolfa Cyf., Talybont, Ceredigion SY24 5AP
e-mail ylolfa@ylolfa.com
website www.ylolfa.com
tel. (01970) 832 304
fax 832 782
isdn 832 813

Snowdonia: Myth and Image

ANTHONY GRIFFITHS

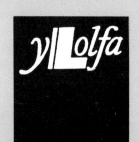

ACKNOWLEDGEMENTS

I would like to thank the following individuals for their assistance in the production of this book.

Brad Banks, my wife Dr Marjorie Griffiths, Jim Perrin, Dr Lleucu Roberts for advice and criticism, Dr Rhiannon Ifans for editing, Michelle Rhodes for typing the early texts, Lynn Symonds of 'Bookcase' Tywyn for her constant encouragement.

The sheet number of the Ordnance Survey 1.50 000 Landranger Map is given with each topic, followed by the relevant six figure grid reference (GR). The four maps needed are sheet numbers 135, 124, 115 and 125. It must be remembered that there are no special rights of access because the land is in the National Park. Rights of way exist but nearly all land in Snowdonia is privately owned.

CONTENTS

FOR
DAVID WILLIAM GRIFFITHS
1946-1981

INTRODUCTION

This book is primarily a photographic study of thirty-two places in Snowdonia. Complementing each image is a concise text, dealing with historical and archaeological facts and curiosities, with an emphasis on Welsh legend and folklore.

Voluntary and governing bodies that control and care for areas of outstanding natural beauty face many cultural, ecological and economic problems. There is often conflict between the needs of those who visit and those who live and work in areas such as Snowdonia. It is not within the scope of this book to touch on these important issues, and anyway, there are far better writers than myself who address such problems. What I present is a personal pilgrimage through a fascinating region, which I have come to know and love since childhood. Starting at the shore of the Dyfi in the south, it finishes in the north, at a lonely church high above Dyffryn Conwy (Conwy Valley). The reader may like to know a little of my life and love of the past.

I was born in 1948 in Bangor, North Wales, but moved shortly after to Aberystwyth when my father was appointed as an archaeologist for the Royal Commission on Ancient Monuments in Wales. As a child I was taken on many digs, and these early outings in the landscape of Wales must have had a deep influence on me. I can still remember family photographs, standing under the massive capstones of cromlechs. Little did I realize then that, years later, I would return to these remote prehistoric sites with my camera.

My father had been a keen climber when he was a student at Bangor in the

1930s and my mother had worked at Ogwen Cottage Youth Hostel, cycling up the Nant Ffrancon pass from Bangor each weekend. They both had a great love of North Wales. We had relatives in Anglesey whom we regularly visited. Returning from these occasions through Snowdonia, my parents would point out their favourite haunts. The names fascinated me: Cwm Idwal, the Devil's Kitchen, Dinas Emrys and Lliwedd. David, my elder brother, had been taken to Cwm Idwal and I remember at bedtime, lying awake in the dark, listening to him describe, in whispers, the Devil's Kitchen.

David's and my first love was the guitar, which we both played in bands around Aberystwyth. After several years hitch-hiking around Europe with my guitar, my wife and I moved to London where, with Paul Darby, I formed the folk duo 'Windfall'.

They were happy times, playing at all the major folk clubs, making many friends, several of whom are now well known performers. Returning to Wales one holiday, my father took my wife and I up Snowdon. I immediately loved hill walking and bought Pouchers' *The Welsh Peaks*, which was very useful, for it introduced me to landscape and mountain photography. With the help of the book I prepared each holiday for a new peak: Pumlumon, Cadair Idris, Tryfan, and got to know a little more about the landscape of my native country. Eventually my love of North Wales was such that we returned to live in Harlech.

Since my return, like my father, I have learnt to rock-climb, discovering the high crags of Glyder Fach, Cwm Cywarch and other climbing areas in Snowdonia. Now that I am close to the mountains, the opportunities to be active and creative are endless. Over the years I have become interested in Welsh prehistory and folklore. And so this, my first book, is a selection of images chosen to reflect and share my love of photography, the past and, of course, Snowdonia.

In the following pages you will meet with mountains, lakes and monuments named after some hero, prince or saint, so why not dedicate a book to the memory of a dear brother? There are times, when, alone on the shore of Llyn Idwal, I see a small figure far across the lake, moving slowly over the grey boulders beneath the Devil's Kitchen, and, like the legend, I hear a whispering voice float over the dark *cwm*.

NOTES ON PHOTOGRAPHY

I would like to say a little about what I consider to be a highly subjective art. My equipment is rather basic. All the photographs in this book were taken with an Olympus OM1n 35mm camera, a discontinued model which can still be purchased at a reasonable price secondhand. Nowadays there are many sophisticated cameras on the market that will do almost everything. They all produce excellent results, but technical ability cannot be learnt on an auto-exposure camera.

There is no mystique about photography, but it is important to learn about lenses and exposure, i.e. aperture, film and shutter speed, which is not too difficult. Once understood, the craft is in its application.

In landscape photography, creativity comes from moving in, and being familiar with the landscape, and developing a deep feeling for a place. It takes time to learn to see, and one must be critical, selective and patient. There are rules of composition but even these have to be broken sometimes. There are hundreds of manuals available from which a lot can be learnt but in the end you have to get out into the landscape if you want results. The important thing is to know what you want to take, and how to go about photographing it. I am learning all the time.

I have three lenses, a 28mm, 50mm and 135mm. Almost all the images were taken on the 28mm wide angle lens. The only filters I use are a skylight to suppress haze, often encountered in the mountains, and a polarizer to eliminate reflections on water and darken the sky. I take every shot with a shutter release cable, on a reliable tripod—an important item—for I use slow slide film, Kodachrome 25, 64 and Fuji 50.

1 THE DYFI ESTUARY

135 GR 610960

The Dyfi Estuary is the natural southern boundary of Snowdonia. The birthplace of Afon Dyfi is the isolated Craiglyn Dyfi cradled below the summit cliffs of Aran Fawddwy. It enters the sea at Aberdyfi and in Welsh folklore the river mouth is associated with the origins of the great Welsh poet Taliesin.

Ceridwen, the goddess of poetry and inspiration, lived with her husband Tegid Foel in Llyn Tegid (Bala Lake). They had two children: a beautiful girl called Ceirwy and Afagddu, who was the ugliest boy in the world. To compensate for the boy's ugliness Ceridwen decided to bestow on him the gift of knowledge by brewing him a magic potion in her cauldron.

The cauldron was watched over and kept simmering for a year and a day by a local boy named Gwion Bach who accidentally spilt three drops of the magic brew on his finger. The servant boy licked his finger and acquired the gift intended for Afagddu. In doing so Gwion realised that Ceridwen intended to kill him after his work was completed.

The boy fled and Ceridwen pursued him. Due to his powers drawn from the potion he changed himself into a hare. Ceridwen changed herself into a greyhound. Gwion plunged into a river and became a fish. Ceridwen became an otter. Gwion leapt out of the water and became a small bird. Ceridwen turned into a hawk. Gwion became a tiny grain of wheat in a barn. Ceridwen became a black hen, scratched the wheat and swallowed him.

Ceridwen transformed herself into her own form and was pregnant of Gwion who was born a fine looking boy. Because of his beauty she had not the heart to kill him so she tied him in a leather bag and threw him into the sea. The boy was caught in a salmon weir at the mouth of Afon Dyfi and rescued from it by Prince Elphin, the nephew of King Maelgwn of Gwynedd.

Prince Elphin reared the child and then renamed him Taliesin, which means 'beautiful brow'. The boy grew up and became the chief bard of Britain in the late sixth century.

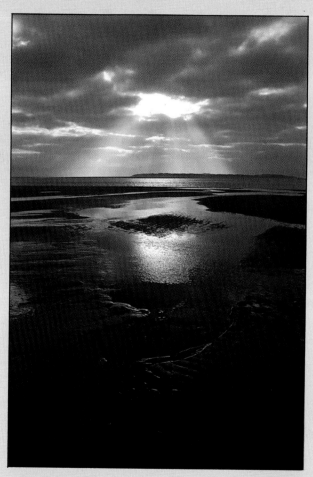

Light on the Dyfi

2 LLYN BARFOG

135 GR 654988

Llyn Barfog (the Bearded Lake), lies in the hilly country above Aberdyfi, its name probably derived from the reeds fringing its shore.

There are some curious local legends here relating to King Arthur whose foster father was named Cynyr Barfog. The *afanc*, a mythical water monster reputed to dwell in the lake, was drawn out by King Arthur and his horses and hurled into Llyn Cau. Close by is a rock called *Carn March Arthur* (the Cairn of Arthur's Stallion), bearing the imprint of the hoof of Arthur's horse.

The most popular legend of the lake is about *Y Fuwch Gyfeiliorn* (the Stray Elfin Cow). Llyn Barfog formed one of the communications between this world and *Annwfn*, the Celtic underworld. *Annwfn* was the dominion of Gwyn ap Nudd and *Gwragedd Annwfn* (Women of the Underworld).

An old farmer from Dysyrnant used to see at eventide on the lake's shore, *Gwragedd Annwfn* with their white hounds and *Gwartheg y Llyn* (the Kine of the Lake). He captured one of the cows and added it to his herd. The farmer was envied in the neighbourhood for the abundance and quality of milk, butter and cheese produced by his herd.

Years passed and the Stray Elfin Cow grew old so the farmer decided to slaughter her. On the day of the killing the farmfold all gathered. The farmer was about to strike the fatal blow with his knife when his arm became paralysed. A piercing cry resounded from the hills around. The gathering looked up and there standing on a rock above Llyn Barfog was a green clad female. In a voice as loud as thunder she called:

> *Dere di felen Einion*
> *Cyrn gyfeiliorn braith y llyn*
> *A'r foel Dodin*
> *Codwch, dowch adre.'*

> 'Come Einion's yellow one
> Stray speckled horns of the lake
> And the hornless Dodin
> Arise and come home.'

The Stray Elfin Cow and all her progeny down to the last generation walked uphill towards the lake with the farmer in breathless pursuit. He stood above the lake and looking down saw the green clad elfin lead the herd into the middle of the lake where they formed a circle around her, tossing their tails. She raised her arms and they all slowly disappeared underwater, leaving only the green and yellow lily pads on the surface of Llyn Barfog.

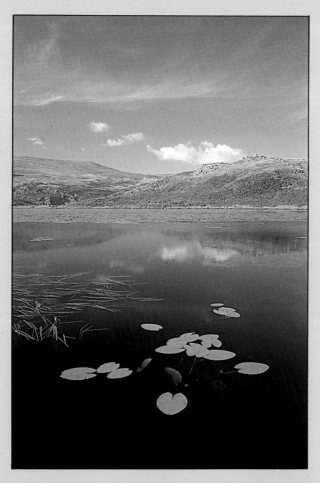

Lily Pads on the Bearded Lake

3 LLANGELYNNIN

124 GR 571071

This ancient church below the road between Tywyn and the village of Llwyngwril is beautifully situated on the gorse clad stone-walled slopes leading down to the boulder clay sea cliffs. There is an air of sanctity about the place, enhanced by the splendid view across the bay of Llŷn and the holy isle of Enlli (Bardsey Island), the resting place of 20,000 saints. The church, and another near Conwy, is dedicated to Saint Celynnin who lived in the seventh century.

Llangelynnin's architecture is rather primitive. From the outside the only distinguishing ecclesiastical feature is the small belfry above the porch. There is a holy water stoup in the wall of the porch made from a large hollowed out pebble which probably came from the beach below. Inside the simple nave and southern porch are rows of oak benches with the names of parishioners painted on them. On the north wall is an interesting double horse bier, *elor feirch*. It has handles at both ends where the horses were harnessed. There are bars in the centre where the coffin was placed. It was used in the past to bring the bodies of the hillfolk down the rough mountain tracks.

Outside the porch entrance is a stone slab with the initials A.W. inscribed on it. This is the grave of Abram Wood, 'King of the Welsh Gypsies', whose descendants were known as *Teulu Abram Wood* (Abram Wood's Family). In the Register, the following is recorded: 'Abram Wood, a travelling gypsy, buried December 13th 1799.'

Abram and his wife Sarah came to Wales from Somerset in the eighteenth century, and the Wood family was renowned for magicianship, fortune telling and for musical gifts. Several Welsh harpists were descendants of Abram Wood among which were John Wood Jones, employed by Lady Llanofer; Jeremiah Wood, harpist at Gogerddan, Cardiganshire and the most famous John Roberts, who formed a family of Welsh harpists known as 'The Original Cambrian Minstrels.'

Abram Wood died in a cowshed on a farm, above the church, and in the gypsy tradition his resting place was described as 'by a little lone, lovely ancient church by the sea.'

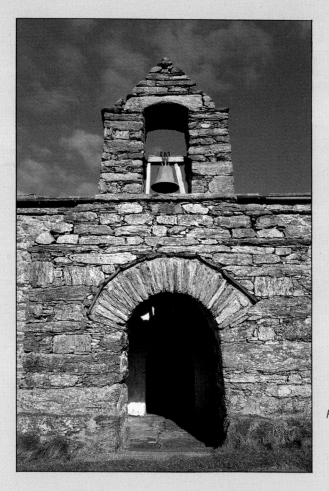

Porch and Belfry, Llangelynnin.

4 CRAIG YR ADERYN

124 GR 643068

The precipitous crag of Craig yr Aderyn is a striking feature in the quiet unspoilt Dysynni valley near Tywyn. Its natural defensive position was an ideal site for the Iron Age fort on its bold summit rising 232 metres above the flat valley floor.

Craig yr Aderyn (Bird Rock), as it is known, is the ancestral breeding ground of the cormorant. Some thirty pairs nest on the high crags of the eastern face above the quarry. Though six miles from the sea it is the only regular inland breeding place of the cormorant. Thomas Pennant's *Tours in Wales* mentions the birds as long ago as 1784 but the colony is probably ancient, going back to the time when the sea washed the base of the buttress. Nowadays, with consent from the landowner, the rock is protected and watched over by the West Wales Naturalist Trust. In the nesting season the birds soar off from the crags to the nearby lakes, rivers and sea in search of food.

The buttresses are now the playground of the rock climber, and the main feature, the spectacular, slightly overhanging, diamond shaped wall only a few yards from the road, has some excellent technical climbing. During the nesting season climbing is forbidden on the higher eastern face.

Many years ago Craig yr Aderyn was a favourite meeting place of the Welsh gypsies, descendants of Abram Wood. They would gather at the foot of the rock in the summer evenings and play their harps and fiddles long into the warm nights.

The foxglove is known in Welsh folklore as *Menyg y Tylwyth Teg* (Fairies' Gloves), also *Menyg Ellyllon* (Elves' Gloves).

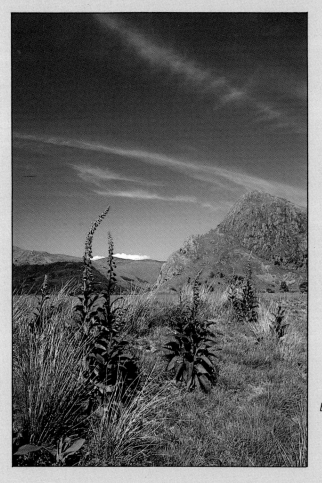

Bird Rock, Dysynni Valley

5 SACRED OAKS

124 GR 667086

The climate in Britain around 3,000 BC was drier and warmer than it is now and much of Snowdonia would have been covered by woods of birch, alder and pine. Remains of these extinct forests may still be seen along parts of coastal Wales.

Gradually the climate got cooler and wetter, creating unfavourable marshy and peaty conditions so that forests retreated from the highlands to lower ground.

Prehistoric man cleared much of the fertile valleys and lowlands and nowadays the principal species of tree in the park is the slowly degenerating sessile oak.

The oak was sacred to the Druids who inhabited Wales some 2,000 years ago and they worshipped at turf altars in clearings of oak groves.

The Druids were an order of priest-philosophers, interested in astronomy and natural science. Their teachings and knowledge were not permitted to be written down so they had a secret form of finger language with letters marked by the tips, joints and bases of fingers and thumb. Communication was made by touching appropriate parts of the one hand with the finger of the other.

In Welsh the word Druid is *Derwydd* and is related to the Greek word, *drus*, an oak.

The oak trees in the photograph grow below the ramparts of Castell y Bere in the Dysynni valley east of Tywyn.

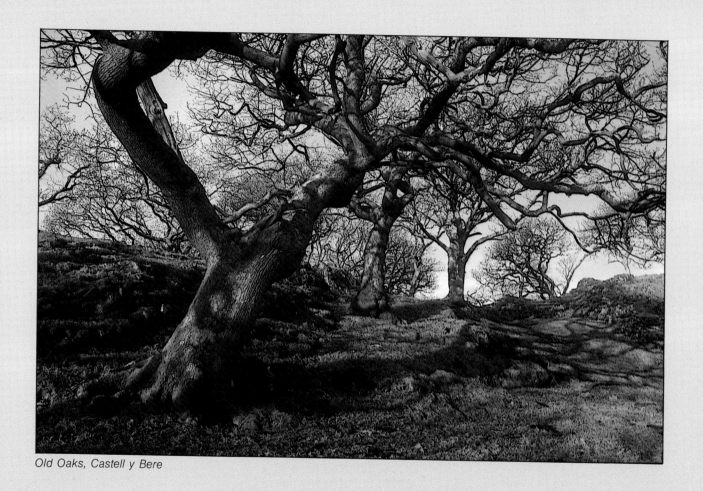

Old Oaks, Castell y Bere

6 CASTELL Y BERE

124 GR 667086

The visitor to North Wales is no doubt familiar with the monumental castles, such as Harlech, Caernarfon and Conwy, built by the English, but Wales too has an architectural heritage of lesser known castles built by the native Princes.

The early Welsh castles were modelled on the conquering Norman earth and timber structures, known as a motte and bailey. The first stone castles were built by Llywelyn ap Iorwerth (Llywelyn Fawr) who ruled the whole of Gwynedd and beyond at the beginning of the thirteenth century. Llywelyn drew up a settlement at Aberdyfi and began a programme of castle building. Among the castles built were Castell y Bere, Dolwyddelan and Dolbadarn.

In *Brut y Tywysogion* (The Chronicle of the Princes) there is a reference to Castell y Bere stating that 'Llywelyn took from Gruffydd (his son) the cantref of Meirionnydd and the commot of Ardudwy. And he began a castle there for himself.' The castle stands on an isolated natural outcrop in the peaceful Dysynni valley, with fine views of Craig yr Aderyn.

By 1255 Llywelyn's grandson, Llywelyn ap Gruffudd, ruled Gwynedd. He refused to pay homage to Edward I and war eventually broke out. Most Welsh castles were besieged and captured and Llywelyn Ein Llyw Olaf was killed at Cilmeri near Builth Wells in 1282.

Shortly afterwards, Castell y Bere, the last Welsh castle, surrendered on 25 April 1283. Its ruins stand today in a picturesque setting, a monument and symbol of Wales' struggle to maintain independence.

In the photograph, in the distance, is the hamlet of Llanfihangel-y-Pennant. Here stands the ruined cottage of Ty'n-y-ddôl, birthplace of Mary Jones who walked barefoot over the mountains to Y Bala to purchase a Welsh Bible. On her arrival the last copy had been sold, so the minister, Thomas Charles, gave her his own. It was this incident that inspired him to form the British and Foreign Bible Society which still possess Mary Jones' Bible.

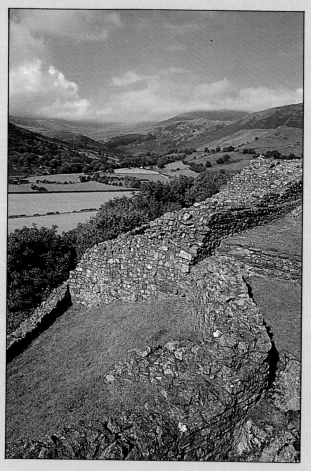

Ramparts, Castell y Bere

7 TAL-Y-LLYN

124 GR 720100

Tal-y-llyn means simply 'the end of the lake'. There is however an older and more descriptive name which is Llyn y Mwyngil, 'the Lake of the Charming Retreat'.

Although shallow and reedy, it has long been a favourite retreat of anglers since the Ty'n y Gornel hotel was built in 1844.

St Mary's Church set at its western corner is the perfect example of a small Welsh church. The present building is about 500 years old, but has undergone many changes. The air 'Cadair Idris' is also known as 'Jenny Jones', who lies buried in the churchyard. Jenny went with her Welsh fusilier husband to Waterloo and was at his side for three days on the battlefield.

The most curious tale relating to Tal-y-llyn concerns the finding of some enormous coffins. Thomas Pennant, the Welsh naturalist and antiquary, published in 1778 his *Tours of Wales*. Whilst visiting Tal-y-llyn he records that in 1684, whilst digging turf at Llwyn Dôl Ithel, a coffin seven feet long was found, nine feet deep in the turf. It was made of deal, carved and gilded at each end. Inside were two skeletons of opposite sex, placed with the head of one parallel to the feet of the other.

The bones were moist and tough and unusually large, the thigh bone measuring 27 inches long. Along the graves and coffin were laid hazel rods with the bark still on them. They were highly preserved due to the quality of the peat.

Pennant supposes that the rods were placed for some superstitious reason, probably to avert the power of witchcraft, and in some parts of the Highlands of Scotland a double hazelnut is placed in the grave for the same purpose.

In the eighteenth century during the restoration of Chester Cathedral, a hazel rod with bark on it was found in the grave of Ranulf Higden, a Benedictine.

The hazel tree and nut appear in Irish folklore and are the symbols and emblems of wisdom and poetic art. In Ireland during Pagan times, a wooden rod was used for measuring corpses and graves. It was an honour to touch the rod, and Pagans used to inscribe on it in Ogham, an early form of writing originating from Southern Ireland in the fourth centry AD. Letters were represented by cutting horizontal and diagonal strokes across the edges of standing stones.

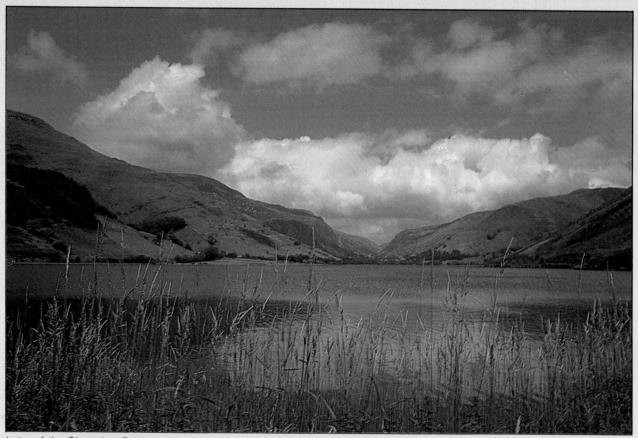

Lake of the Charming Retreat

8 CADAIR IDRIS

124 GR 711130

Cadair Idris, along with Yr Wyddfa (Snowdon) and Pumlumon, is one of the three principal mountains of Wales. It has long been a favourite of mountain walkers because of its lofty position, accessibility and the relatively easy paths to its summit, Pen y Gadair.

There are three lakes north of the summit, Llyn y Gadair, Llyn Gafr and to the east the tiny and rarely visited Llyn Aran, lying close below, the flanks of Mynydd Moel. Cadair Idris' most impressive lake is Llyn Cau situated under the towering crags of Mynydd Pencoed and Pen y Gadair. It would be hard to find another lake in Wales to excel it for its wild and magnificent setting.

Tradition tells us that Idris was probably Idris ap Gwyddno, a seventh century Prince of Meirionnydd who fought an important battle against the invading Irish.

Legend has it that Idris Gawr was a giant who liked to study the stars from his high throne. The mountain boasts several legends, the most popular claiming that those who spend a night alone on the summit of the mountain will come down either blind, a madman or a poet. This legend was transferred to Cadair Idris and belongs to a rock called Maen-du'r Arddu on Yr Wyddfa.

At the top of the Tal-y-llyn pass is a reedy hollow that was once a lake called Llyn y Tri Greuenyn ('The Lake of the Three Pebbles'). The pebbles are three huge boulders said to have been flung out of the shoe of Idris Gawr.

The most interesting story of Cadair Idris is associated with *Cŵn Annwfn* ('The Hounds of the Underworld').

They were a pack of white hounds with red ears led by Gwyn ap Nudd, the king of the *Tylwyth Teg* ('fair people' or 'fairies'). Their howling was a foreboding of death and whenever they approached, birds stopped singing and other dogs fled in terror.

The legend says that a minstrel called Ned Pugh was last seen in the twilight of a misty hallowe'en entering a wonderful cave at Talyclegyr near Shrewsbury. He had with him a fiddle on which he began to play an air called 'Ffarwel Ned Pugh'. The tune 'Farewell Ned Pugh' is retained in Welsh folk music to this day. While he was playing he disappeared into Annwfn, the underworld. In Annwfn he exchanged his fiddle for a bugle and became chief huntsman to Gwyn ap Nudd. Every hallowe'en he may be seen cheering *Cŵn Annwfn* as they hunt the souls of the departed over the mountain of Cadair Idris.

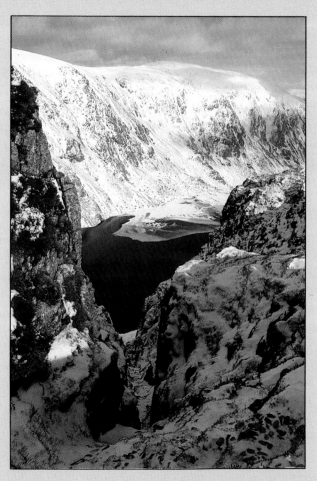

Llyn Cau, Cadair Idris

9 STANDING STONES

124 GR 652133

Standing stones are numerous throughout Britain and in Wales this type of monument is known as a *Maen Hir* or Long Stone. Another name for them is *Maen Gobaith* (Guide Stone), and *Maen Terfyn* (Boundary Stone).

Their prehistoric origins are not certain but many are linked and sited close to the trackways, cairns and burial mounds of the Bronze Age around 2,000 BC. Most remain in their original position but some have been incorporated into farm buildings and walls or used as gateposts. The Tresgawen stone in Anglesey illustrates how man has used the stone over the centuries. It originally served as an ancient marker, then inscribed in Latin to Christianize it to prevent Pagan worship, and subsequently found in the ruins of Capel Bronwen where it has been used as a cattle rubbing post. It then had the top broken off and was drilled for a gatepost, and later served as a chopping block near Llantrisant, before being removed to Llangwyllog.

In a 'land of mystery' such as Wales, it would seem natural that much folklore and superstition have surrounded standing stones. In parts of Wales some stones are composed of a small lumpy material called pudding stone which is believed to breed. They are also known as 'mother stones' or 'growing stones'. It is sometimes said that stones have the ability to expand and contract and even amble off for a moonlight walk down to the river for a drink!

Many standing stones are believed to have been thrown by giants, King Arthur or the Druids, and any attempts to move them will bring on an imminent thunderstorm or downpour. Folklore has attributed them with healing powers, and stones with holes in them are reported to affect marvellous cures if athritic limbs are inserted. Recently, several theories have developed about standing stones transmitting energy and shock waves when encircled or touched.

The *Maen Hir* in the photograph lies close to the prehistoric trackway known as *Ffordd Ddu* (The Dark Road). It is one of thirteen recorded stones sited along the mountain trackway whose route originally started at the haven of the Broadwater north of Tywyn. The track runs north of Afon Dysynni to Llwyngwril, and then gently climbs the slopes overlooking the Mawddach towards Cregennen, crossing the flanks of Cadair Idris. The route eventually found its way to the Severn and the Cotswolds, the gateway to Wessex and the Thames Valley.

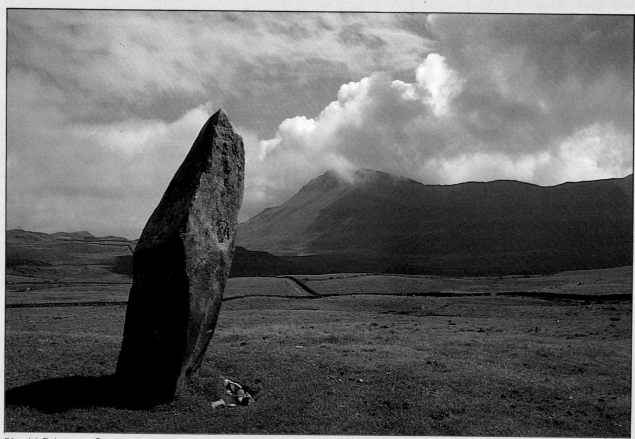

Ffordd Ddu near Cregennen

10 LLYN GWERNAN

124 GR 705160

'The lake of the Alder Tree' is a reedy lake two miles south west of Dolgellau. It lies on a marshy level beside the minor road to Tŷ Nant car park, the starting point for the pony track ascent of Cadair Idris.

The line of Ffordd Ddu would have passed close to the lake and it is interesting to note that the two gold torcs found in Snowdonia lie close to prehistoric trackways. One was found near Harlech, the other by Gilfachwydd farmhouse not far from Llyn Gwernan.

The farmer's wife had noticed the torc in the ground but had ignored it as she did not know what it was. In 1823 the son of a former rector of Dolgellau was walking through the heather and kicked what he took to be a piece of straw. It proved to be a gold torc of Irish import, forty two inches long, weighing eight and a half ounces.

There is a remnant of a 'kelpie' story connected with Llyn Gwernan. The 'kelpie' was a water spirit who delighted in drowning travellers.

A man was returning from Dolgellau at dusk to the village of Llanegryn. As he walked alongside the lake he heard a voice crying out from the water:

'Daeth yr awr   'The hour is come
ond ni ddaeth y dyn.'   but the man is not.'

The startled villager continued on his way and shortly met a crazed looking man wearing nothing but his shirt. The madman rushed towards the lake but the villager could not prevent him from being claimed by the lake spirit.

There are some interesting examples of river spirits claiming victims in Scottish folklore:

'Blood thirsty Dee   'Tweed said to Till
Each year needs three   What gars ye rin sae still?
But bonny Don   Till said to Tweed
She needs none. .   Though ye rin wi speed
                        An I rin slaw
                        Yet whar ye droon ae man
                        I droon twa.'

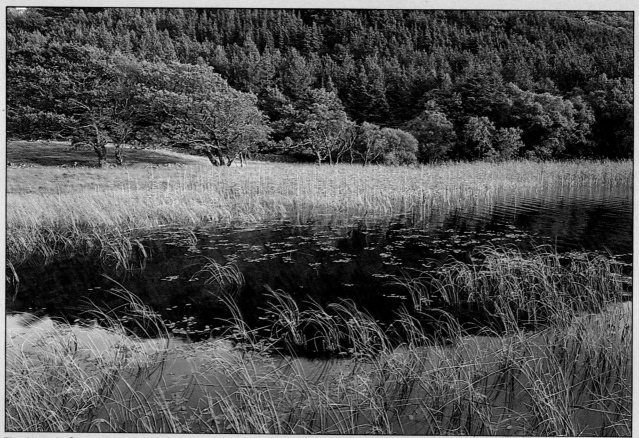

The Hour is Come—but the Man is Not

11 LLYN TEGID

125 GR 920350

Llyn Tegid or Bala Lake was known in the thirteenth century as Pembelmere, an important fishery belonging to the Abbot and Monks of Basingwerk, a Cistercian monastery in Flintshire.

Tradition has it that the lake is the watery tomb of the palaces of iniquity, and on quiet moonlit nights boatmen have heard a feeble voice saying *'Dial a ddaw'* ('Vengeance will come'). Another voice is heard asking, *'Pa bryd y daw?'* ('When will it come?'), then the first voice replies, *'Yn y drydedd genhedlaeth'* ('In the third generation').

'Long ago a cruel prince lived in a palace in the area. He often heard a voice in the breeze saying, "Vengeance will come," but always laughed the threat away. One night, to honour the birth of his son, the prince invited a humble harper to perform at a grand banquet.

'As the evening wore on the revellers got more and more drunk and the harper, reluctant to carry on, sought the solitude of a quiet corner. Whilst resting he heard a whispering voice say "Be gone, Vengeance". He turned and saw a small bird hovering above his harp crying again, "Be gone, Vengeance".

'Following as fast as he could the bird led the harper out of the palace into the dark stormy night. Onwards they fled towards a hill, until, too exhausted to continue, the harper fell to the ground. He lay there in the dark sheltering beneath a hedge, but could no longer hear the bird's warning voice. The storm continued, but being tired he slept on through the night to awake in the dawn to a strange calm. He looked down the slope towards the grand palaces, but all had vanished and had been replaced by a large lake, with a harp floating on its quiet surface.'

Another legend says 'that there was once a holy well in the centre of Ffynnongower, near Llangower, which was guarded by a water spirit. The well had a lid, and the people collecting their daily water were obliged to replace the covering every night, lest the spirit became angry. One night someone forgot to replace the lid, and the villagers awoke to a terrible deluge and fled for safety up the higher slopes of the mountain. At the break of day they looked down and all they could see was a large lake. Sometimes on a clear day you can see the roofs and chimneys of Ffynnongower far below in the green depths.'

Given the recurring theme in Welsh folklore of the drowned village, it is a strange irony that nowadays, with the loss of Welsh communities due to the development of modern reservoirs, tradition is gradually turning into reality.

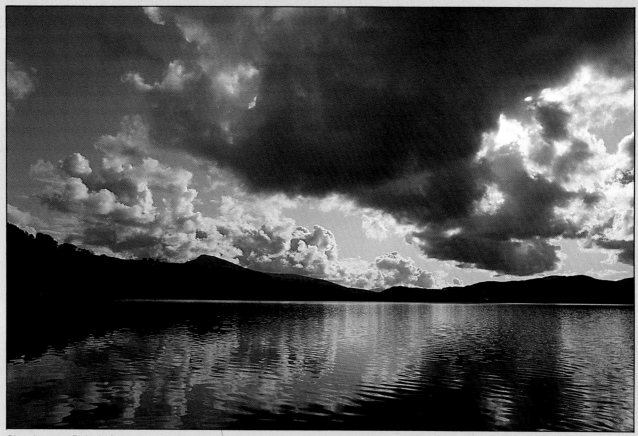

Clouds over Bala Lake

12 BWLCH Y GROES

125 GR 863223 + GR 914233

At 546 metres above sea level Bwlch y Groes (Pass of the Cross), between Llanuwchlyn and Dinas Mawddwy, is the highest road in North Wales. The top of Bwlch y Groes is a wild tussocky landscape, giving superb views of Llyn Tegid (Bala Lake), the Arennig Mountains and nearby, the dark rugged skyline and eastern wall of the Aran mountains.

Bwlch y Groes owes its name to a great crucifix that once stood at the top. It could be seen standing out against the sky, and cheered weary travellers on the ascent. Thomas Pennant remarks that a cross stood here to 'excite the thanksgiving of travellers for having so well accomplished their arduous journey,' and described the mountain crossing as one of the most terrible in North Wales. George Borrow too crossed Bwlch y Groes and mentions a turf pyramid with a pole in it. Nowadays a new wooden cross has been placed at the junction of the mountain road to Llyn Efyrnwy (Lake Vyrnwy).

Aran Fawddwy at 907 metres is the highest mountain in southern Snowdonia and its summit cairn is said to have been erected by the men of Dinas Mawddwy. Wrongly thinking that Cadair Idris was two metres higher, they unnecessarily built the cairn to raise the height of the mountain.

The Aran Mountains have legends associated with King Arthur, who while crossing Bwlch y Groes to visit Myrddin (Merlin), cut a walking stick from the hedgerows. In the 'Faerie Queen', the poet Spenser says that Arthur was educated at the foot of the Aran mountains, and that Arthur and Myrddin sought solitude in a cave 'under Raurans mossie hoar'.

Arthur fought a mighty battle at the top of Bwlch y Groes with the giant Rhita Gawr. Rhita had a robe adorned with the beards of men he had slain. One day he met Arthur and wished to add Arthur's beard to his garment to make a collar. Arthur, reluctant to part with his long golden beard, fought the giant, and in his victory flung Rhita down the hillside almost to Afon Twrch where he lies buried. Arthur commanded each one of his men to place a stone on the giant and that is how the mountain was created.

There is a rough track leading down to the farm of Tan-y-bwlch which is called Rhiw Barfau (Beard Hill). Near the farm gate is a long narrow trench surrounded by boulders, wherein is supposed to be the body of Rhita. Arthur is also said to have buried the giant on the summit of Aran Benllyn, a mile north of Aran Fawddwy. Snowdon, whose original name was Yr Wyddfa Fawr (The Great Tomb), also claims to be the grave of Rhita Gawr.

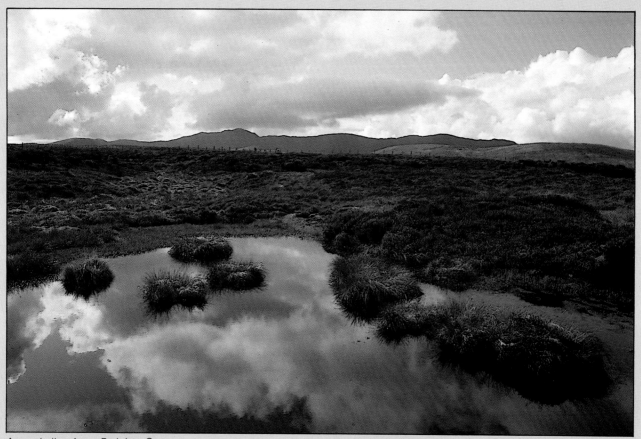

Aran skyline from Bwlch y Groes

13 CYMER ABBEY

124 GR 726195

Cymer Abbey was founded by the Cistercian order in the late twelfth century. Its siting in the peaceful upper reaches of Afon Mawddach, at its confluence with Afon Wnion, gave rise to the name *Kymer deu ddyfyr* (the meeting of two waters).

Llywelyn Fawr, a patron of monasticism, and the greatest ruler of medieval Wales, granted the Abbey a charter in 1209. Monastic life was self-contained. The monks had a good trade in dairy farming and owned one of the best salmon pools in the area, at Llanelltyd bridge. The Abbey held the churches of Llanelltyd, Llanfachreth and Llanegryn and had several granges in the locality. The charter mentions the rights for 'fishing and staking of nets in rivers, pools and shores', also, 'to dig and carry away metals in mountains', though there is no evidence of their prospecting.

In 1890 two men from Dolgellau prospecting for gold on the slopes of Y Garn to the north stumbled upon some badly discoloured metal objects. They were a silver gilt chalice and paten from Cymer, evidently hidden by the monks at the time of the Abbey's fate in 1536 when Henry VIII passed the act of the 'dissolution of the monasteries.'

Ignorant of their value, they were sold locally for fifty shillings, later selling at Christie's for £710. The treasures then exchanged hands for £3,000 and in 1910 were bequeathed to the Crown, who eventually donated them to the National Museum of Wales.

The flower in the foreground growing in the Abbey's drainage system is the Monkey Flower. It was originally a native of the Aleutian Islands in the Bering Sea. The plant was naturalized in Wales in the early nineteenth century, and so named because the flowers resemble little monkeys' faces.

The ruins of Cymer Abbey are now maintained by Cadw, Welsh Historic Monuments.

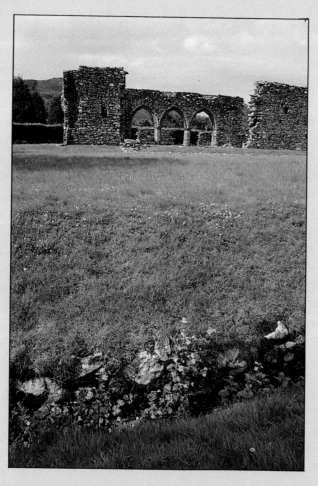

Monkey Flowers, Cymer Abbey

14 LLYN IRDDYN

124 GR 630220

The ancient *cantref* (division of land) of Ardudwy between the rivers Glaslyn and Mawddach is bordered in the west by the sea and the Rhinog mountains, and in the east by the Trawsfynydd plain. The core of this region is called the Harlech Dome, where some of the oldest rocks in Britain can be found.

It is a wild stony heathery landscape of rough mountains and hidden lakes with intriguing names such as *Llyn y Morynion* (the Maidens' Lake); *Gloywlyn* (the Bright Lake), known locally as *Llyn Maneg* (Glove Lake) due to its shape resembling a hand, and *Llyn Irddyn* (the Priest's Lake), traditionally associated with the Druids.

Llyn Irddyn is a small lake lying close below the rocky west slopes of Llawlech, the long ridge leading up from Barmouth to Diffwys, the most southerly peak of Y Rhiniog.

There is a story hereabouts passed down in the oral tradition, that it is wise to shun the edge of the lake and walk on the grass in order to avoid mischievous fairies. It was believed that the fairies could not harm or molest anyone who touched grass. The fairies used to love to visit the earth and seize a mortal and ask whether he would travel above wind, mid wind, or below wind. Above wind was a stormy passage, below wind was through the thicket and undergrowth, so mid wind was the safest course to take. The way to secure a safe passage was to catch hold of the grass, for the *Tylwyth Teg* had not the power to destroy or even injure a blade of grass.

In certain parts of Cardiganshire boys played a type of tig or touchwood game. Any child wanting a stoppage of the game picked a blade of grass which gave him a temporary spell of security, before the game recommenced.

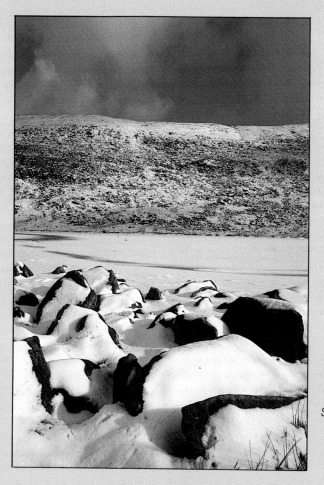

Snowy shore of the Priest's Lake

15 DROVERS' WAYS

124 GR 635235

The old trackways of Ardudwy were later used by the Romans, becoming in the Middle Ages winding pack-horse trails, then Drovers' Ways, and by the eighteenth century were serving as coach roads.

The drovers were the men whose job was the driving of the cattle, sheep, pigs and geese from Wales to markets and fairs in England. Tough, coarse, and independent men with a reputation for drinking, the numerous inns which were their overnight halts still bear the name of 'Drovers' Arms'. Travelling far and wide, bringing back stories and songs from distant towns, they were often regarded as slightly romantic figures.

They stuck to regular ways, and in northern Snowdonia the old drove routes went through Snowdon's passes, converging at the vale of Ffestiniog. The way then ascended, crossing the remote marsh of Y Migneint, eventually heading towards Wrecsam, a main stopping place near the border.

In the south, several routes crossed from Harlech to Trawsfynydd and Dolgellau, through the wild passes of Y Rhinog, heading for Y Bala.

Pont Sgethin between Dyffryn Ardudwy and Bont Ddu is a beautiful example of a small stone bridge forming part of the old coach road from London to Harlech. The drovers would have crossed the bridge *en route* to Dolgellau. It stands in a remote marshy valley straddling Afon Sgethin, below the hill of Moelfre. There is a fairy story familiar to the shepherds of Ardudwy about Moelfre.

'A farmer married one of the *Tylwyth Teg* on condition that he did not touch her with iron. They had dwelt happily together for years on the slopes of Moelfre. One summer day whilst shearing his sheep, the farmer absentmindedly put the *gwelle* (shears) in his wife's hand. On looking up she instantly disappeared.'

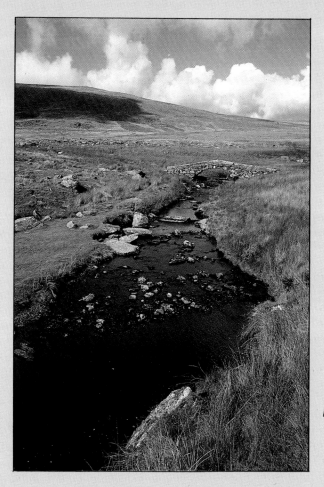

Pont Sgethin and Moelfre skyline

16 ARDUDWY'S ANTIQUITIES

124 GR 731311

For a walker with a love of the past, the Ardudwy area is unsurpassed. Archaeologically it is one of the most important areas in Britain, for here are to be found the most striking collection of chambered tombs, cairns and cromlechs.

Many ancient trackways cross the landscape dating from the Bronze Age up to medieval times. The two prehistoric pathways in the south of Snowdonia started at the natural harbours of the Broadwater near Tywyn, and the mouth of the Artro at Ynys Gragen (Shell Island), near Llanbedr.

Prehistoric man landed at Aber Artro, and a trackway with some twelve recorded standing stones runs from the river mouth north eastwards, through the wild country of the Rhinog mountains. Before the pathway drops down into Cwm Moch, it passes the impressive cairn of Bryn Cader Faner. The burial cairn has a circle of fifteen upright stones leaning outwards, and from a distance its unusual appearance on the skyline represents a giant coronet. The track crosses the Roman road Sarn Helen above Bronaber, then drops into the valley of the Afon Cain. Here stands Llech Idirs, (Idris' Stone), 3.2 metres high, the finest monolith to be found in Snowdonia. The standing stone inspired a local poet to write:

Samson Gawr	The giant Samson
Daflodd y garreg fawr	Threw the big stone
O ben Cader Idris	From the top of Cadair Idris
I gaeau Llech Idris.	To the fields of Llech Idris.

Recent excavation by archaeologists from Plas Tan y Bwlch, the National Park study centre at Maentwrog, unearthed a Roman tile factory at the foot of the stone. Not far from Llech Idris, surrounded by railings, lies the medieval grave of Porius. There is a Latin inscription on the grave stone, probably inscribed by a monk from Cymer Abbey. It reads, 'Porius lies here in the tomb. He was a plain man.' The stone is a replica: the original is to be found in the National Museum of Wales at Cardiff.

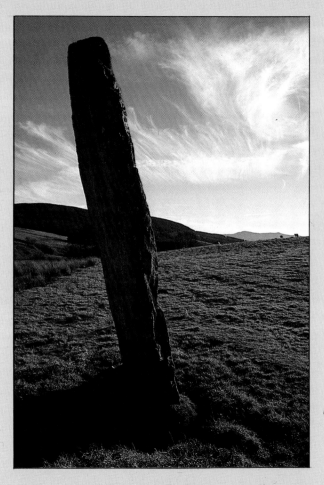

Llech Idris, Stone of the Giant

17 ARENNIG FAWR

124 GR 827370

The twin peaks of Arennig Fawr and Arennig Fach dominate the desolate landscape between Y Bala and Blaenau Ffestiniog. These isolated moorlands are the least frequented parts of Snowdonia.

George Borrow walking through Wales almost 150 years ago remarked that 'Arennig is certainly barren enough, for there is something majestic in its huge bulk. Of all the hills which I saw in Wales none made a greater impression on me.'

Some sixty years later the gaunt mountain held the same fascination for the Welsh painters Augustus John and James Innes who rented a cottage nearby at Nant Ddu. Innes had an almost spiritual obsession with the mountain, and his paintings reveal the powerful appeal of the Welsh landscape. He buried a casket of love letters on the summit cairn which nowadays has a memorial to the crew of eight Americans who in 1943 crashed their Flying Fortress just below the summit.

A mile to the east of Arennig Fawr below the rocky spur of Pen Tyrau is the lonely dark lake of Llyn Arennig Fawr. The lake has a legend similar to that of Llyn Barfog.

'Many years ago a shepherd of Hafod y Garreg was tending his flock on the lonely shore of Llyn Arennig Fawr. In the rushes he saw a slender strong calf, and wondered how it came to be there, as at that time of year cattle were not allowed near the lake. He took the calf home and reared it into a fine looking bull. The cattle of Hafod y Garreg became the wonder and admiration of all the neighbourhood. One afternoon in June the shepherd saw a little fat old man, sitting on a rock near the lake playing a pipe. The little man stood up and called the cows by their names:

'Mulican, Molican, Malen, Mair
Dowch adre'r awrhon ar fy nghair'
'Mulican, Molican, Malen, Mair
Come home now upon my word'

The whole herd ran towards the old man who led them into the lake. Nothing more was seen or heard of them, and it is believed that they were the cattle of the *Tylwyth Teg*.'

In Wales the fairies have at least three common names. The *Tylwyth Teg* (Fair Tribe), is the most common and they, unlike goblins are fair, enchanting and handsome. *Bendith y Mamau* (the Mother's Blessing), is another name, which is not easy to explain, but may reflect a memory of the Mother Goddess, a feature of Pagan Celtic religion. Another name given to fairies is *Ellyll* (Elves).

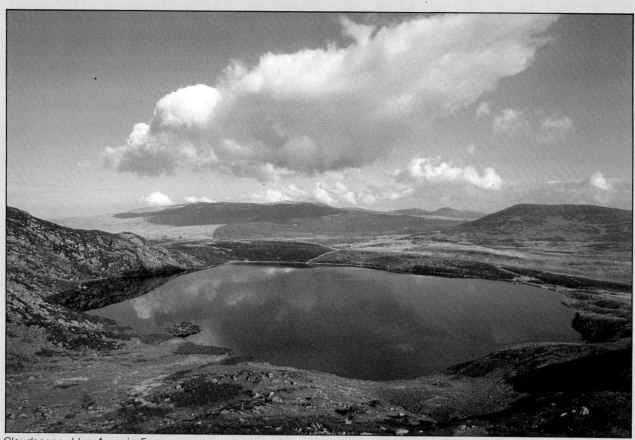

Cloudscape, Llyn Arennig Fawr

18 TOMEN Y MUR

124 GR 705387

The conspicuous 'motte' known as Tomen y Mur, on the bleak hilltop a mile east of Trawsfynydd power station, was probably formed in the early twelfth century. It stands within the walls of one of the most interesting Roman forts in Wales. Sarn Helen runs north and south from the fort, and several military earthworks lie close by. There is also a small amphitheatre, the only one known to exist at a Roman auxiliary fort in Britain.

The site of the fort has been identified as the palace of *Mur Castell* (Castle Wall), mentioned in the tale of Math, son of Mathonwy, the fourth branch of the Mabinogion.

It was the home of the legendary flower maiden Blodeuwedd, and Lleu Llaw Gyffes.

Arianrhod, Lleu's mother, had put a curse on her son that he would never marry a mortal woman. The magicians Math and Gwydion fashioned for Lleu a maiden made from broom, meadowsweet and blossoms of oak. She was named Blodeuwedd, which means 'flower face'.

One day Gronw Pebr, lord of Penllyn, visited Mur Castell during Lleu's absence. Blodeuwedd and Gronw became lovers and conspired to kill Lleu. He could not be killed inside or out, on horseback or on foot, but only on a Sunday by a spear that had taken a whole year in the making.

Gronw set about fashioning the weapon, while Blodeuwedd deceived Lleu into telling her how his death could be brought about. One Sunday on the banks of Afon Cynfal, he showed her that he had to stand with one foot on the edge of a cauldron with a thatched roof, while the other foot rested on the back of a buck.

Gronw was lying in wait and hurled the spear into Lleu's side. The shaft broke off but the head remained in. Lleu immediately changed into an eagle, and flew off with a terrible scream.

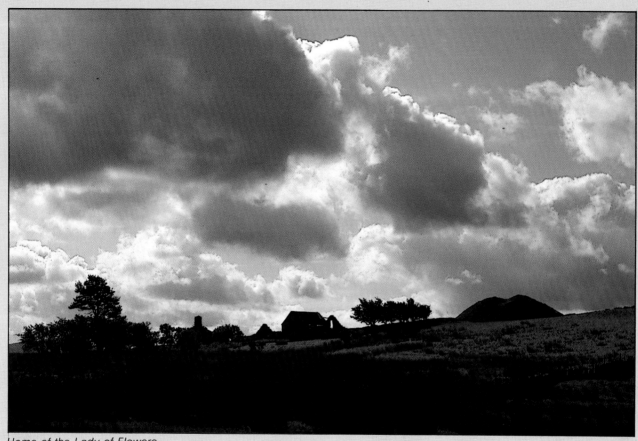

Home of the Lady of Flowers

19 HUW LLWYD'S PULPIT

124 GR 702413

The source of Afon Cynfal lies high up on the bleak moor of Y Migneint east of Ffestiniog. Near Pont yr Afon Gam the stream plunges dramatically into the splendid waterfall of Rhaeadr y Cwm, then winds its way down through Cwm Cynfal into a damp, vegetated, water-worn gorge just south of Ffestiniog.

In the bed of the river near Rhaeadr Cynfal stands a tall, fern-clad pillar of rock known as 'Huw Llwyd's Pulpit'. Huw was a local poet, a keen huntsman and a much respected *dyn hysbys* (soothsayer). He claimed to foretell future events, especially with regard to love and death, and people from North Wales sought his counsel at his pulpit where he delivered his nocturnal sermons.

During one of his speeches he was interrupted and insulted by a farmer. Huw, deeply offended, pronounced a curse on the man who met with nothing but disaster and misery for a whole year. The unfortunate farmer eventually begged Huw's forgiveness, and his circumstances and sufferings were removed.

There is a story relating to a dark pool near the rock called *Llyn Pont Rhyd Ddu* (The Lake by the Bridge of the Black Ford). While Huw lay dying he requested his daughter to throw his books of magic into the pool. Three times she pretended to dispense with the precious volumes, until Huw said he would not die peacefully unless she did as instructed. She hurled the books from the top of the gorge and a hand came out of the water and grasped them, drawing them down into the dark depths of Afon Cynfal. Shortly afterwards Huw Llwyd died in peace.

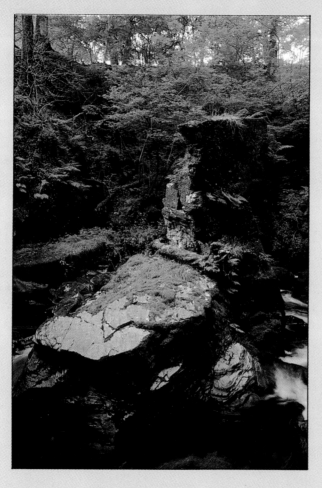

Huw's fern clad Pillar

20 LLYN Y DYWARCHEN

115 GR 560535

The 'Lake of the Turf Island' to the west of Rhyd Ddu was first noted by Giraldus in 1188. In his journey through Wales, he mentions the lake as having 'a floating island on it, which is often driven from one side to the other by the force of the winds.'

In 1698 the astronomer Halley pushed it out from the bank, and swam out to it to satisfy his curiosity that it did float. The island has long since disappeared, and the rocky heather-clad islet visible today is often wrongly mistaken for the once famous floating island.

On the shore beneath Clogwyn y Garreg is a ruined cottage called *Llwyn y Forwyn* (the Maiden's Grove), of which there is a legend.

'One misty day a young shepherd from Drws y Coed was working on the mountain slopes when he beheld the most beautiful girl he had ever seen. Her name was Bella and she was one of the *Tylwyth Teg* (the Fair Folk). They fell in love and used to meet secretly by the shore of Llyn y Dywarchen at a place called Llwyn y Forwyn. They wished to wed but needed the consent of the maiden's father. One moonlit night all three agreed to meet. The youth waited but Bella and her father did not appear until the moon had sunk behind the mountain of Y Garn. When they arrived the old man spoke, "Thou shalt have my daughter on condition that thou do not strike her with iron." Bella and the shepherd were happily married, but alas the sweet cannot be had without the bitter. One day whilst out on horseback by the marshy shore of Llyn y Gader, Bella's horse sank up to its belly in the bog. The husband got her safely off the horse and after a long struggle managed to get the horse out safely on to firm ground. He lifted Bella on to his own horse, but in his haste whilst trying to get her foot in the stirrups, the iron part touched her knee. On the way home several of the *Tylwyth Teg* began to appear and the sound of much singing could be heard. By the time the party reached Drws y Coed she had disappeared and it was supposed that Bella had fled to Llwyn y Forwyn, to the Fairy Kingdom below.

'It was the fairy law that Bella could not now frequent the earth and live with an earthly being, so with her mother's help she invented a way of avoiding the one thing and securing the other. A great turf was set to float on Llyn y Dywarchen and on it Bella would sit and converse with her lover on the shore. It was by this means that they lived together until the shepherd of Drws y Coed finally died.'

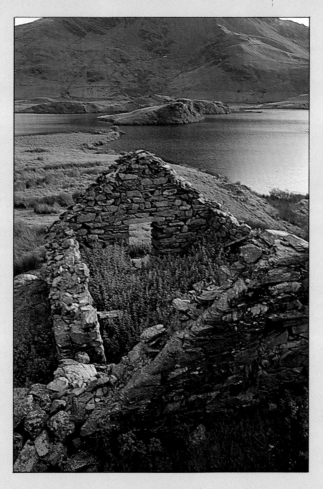

Lake of the Floating Island

21 DYFFRYN NANTLLE

115 GR 551527

Dyffryn Nantlle (Nantlle Valley) runs from the slate quarrying village of Nantlle towards Rhyd Ddu, through the steep pass of Drws-y-coed (the Door of the Wood). The south side of the valley is flanked by the splendid peaks of the Nantlle ridge, popular to walkers, which terminates in the steep arete of Y Garn, guarding the head of the pass. Nantlle is the Nantlleu mentioned in the Mabinogion, and continues the tale of Lleu Llaw Gyffes, who had turned into a wounded eagle.

Gwydion, much grieved by his nephew's disappearance set out to search for Lleu. He traversed the whole of Gwynedd, then Powys, until he came to Arfon, where he learnt of a mysterious sow that wandered off from the sty each morning. Gwydion followed the sow to a valley called Nantlleu, where it rested beneath the boughs of an oak to feed on rotten flesh and maggots. On the topmost branch perched an eagle and each time it shook, the flesh fell from its decaying body. Gwydion stood beneath the boughs and sang an *englyn*. The eagle came down to a branch in the middle of the tree. Gwydion sang another *englyn*, at which the eagle landed on the lowest branch. On singing a third time the bird alighted on his lap. Gwydion struck it with his magic wand, transforming Lleu back into his own likeness.

After his health was restored, Lleu, hungry for revenge, sought out Gronw who offered land and gold in compensation for the injury he had inflicted. Lleu refused, stating that he would only accept that he and Gronw return to the spot where he was smitten. There, by the river, they should change places, so that Gronw would now receive the blow. Gronw begged that a stone be placed between him and the spear. The request was granted, and Lleu took aim, piercing the stone, breaking Gronw's back and killing him. The stone is said to be still on the banks of Afon Cynfal with a hole through it. It is known as *Llech Ronw* (Gronw's Stone).

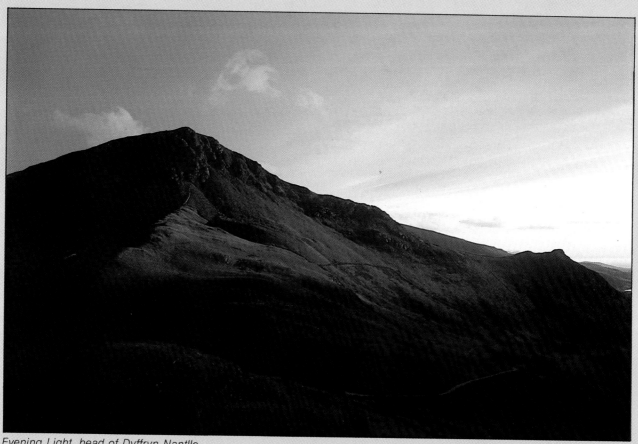

Evening Light, head of Dyffryn Nantlle

22 LLYN Y MORYNION

124 GR 737424

This large peaty lake, two miles east of Ffestiniog, is not to be confused with a lake of the same name in the Rhinog mountains.

The 'Lake of the Maidens' lies high up, offering some unusual views of the Moelwyn peaks from its western shore, giving an almost Hebridean atmosphere to the place. There are two legends relating to its name *Morynion*. The first concerns the flight, and eventual fate, of Blodeuwedd and her maidens of Ardudwy.

After Lleu Llaw Gyffes returned to Ardudwy, Gwydion sought to punish Blodeuwedd for her dishonour and travelled to Mur Castell. Blodeuwedd heard of his coming and fled with her maidens northwards across Afon Cynfal. Through fear they kept looking backwards and stumbled into the lake, where they all drowned apart from Blodeuwedd.

Gwydion caught up with her but not wishing to slay her he transformed her into an owl, the enemy of all birds. She was ordered never to show her face in daylight and thereafter for that reason the owl was known as Blodeuwedd (Flower Face).

The other better known legend has influences of the Sabine women in Roman myth.

The Men of Ardudwy raided Dyffryn Clwyd, carrying off the fairest of the maidens. On their return they camped on the banks of the lake. The men of Clwyd followed and a bloody battle ensued were all the men of Ardudwy were slain. The maidens, who had become enraptured wth their captors, were grief-stricken and in their despair flung themselves into the dark waters of the lake.

A mile to the west of Llyn Morynion is a spot, crossed by Sarn Helen, which is known in tradition as *Beddau Gwŷr Ardudwy* (The graves of the Men of Ardudwy). Nothing is visible of the graves nowadays but there are several references to them by antiquarian travellers. The earliest mention is by the great collector of Welsh manuscripts, Robert Vaughan of Hengwrt, Dolgellau (1592-1666).

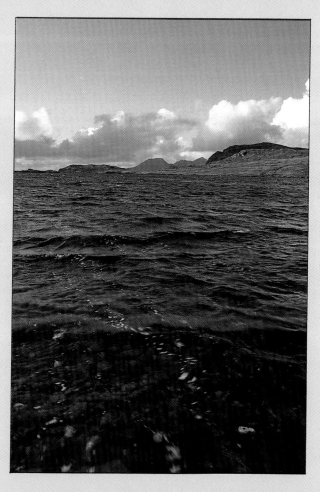

Lake of the Maidens

23 DOLWYDDELAN

115 GR 722523

Dolwyddelan (The Little Irishman's Meadow) which could also be derived from *Dolydd Elan* (Elan's Meadows) after Elen Lwyddog (heroine of the dream of Macsen Wledig in the Mabinogion) stands at the junction of two ancient routes. Sarn Helen, from Tomen y Mur in the south, came down Cwm Penamnen, and a medieval track ran west over the mountains through Bwlch y Rhediad to Nant Gwynant. The village has two fine antiquities of note—its castle and its church.

The old church, encircled by yew trees, was built in the sixteenth century by Maredudd ap Ieuan, ancestor of the Wynns of Gwydir. Inside the slate-floored building is a Gothic wood screen and some fragments of medieval glass. The roof is made from thick slates laid on a bed of sphagnum moss, known as *cerrig mwsog* (moss stones), a rare feature nowadays of Snowdonia's churches. Its finest treasure is *Cloch Wyddelan*, a small battered bronze handbell of early Celtic design.

According to tradition it was dug up nearby at Bryn y Bedd (Hill of the Grave), where once stood an earlier church.

The ruins of the castle stand on a rocky knoll a mile west of the village. Its setting is impressive, situated below the rugged mountain slopes leading up to the shapely peak of Moel Siabod. The castle's main feature, the splendid rectangular tower keep of Norman style, was built by Llywelyn Fawr in the late twelfth century, and is his supposed birthplace. The keep replaced an earlier structure built on an elevated knoll in the valley just below.

The site was strategically important as it guarded the eastern approach from Dyffryn Conwy, and also the way west over Bwlch Gorddinan (the Crimea Pass) into Meirionydd. Dolwyddelan was captured in January 1283 by Edward I, shortly after the death of Llywelyn ap Gruffudd. The castle is now in the care of Cadw, Welsh Historic Monuments.

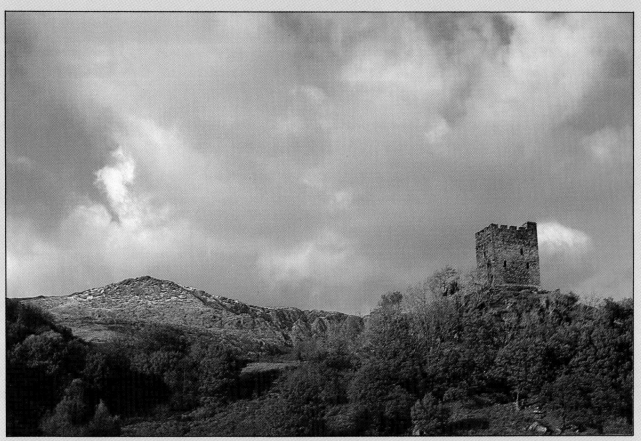

Castell Dolwyddelan and Moel Siabod

24 DINAS EMRYS

115 GR 606493

The conical wooded hill known as the 'Fortress of Ambrosius' is just below the outlet of Llyn Dinas, one and a half miles north east of Beddgelert.

It was to this mystical spot that the Welsh born Gwrtheyrn (Vortigern), King of Britain, retreated from the invading Saxons. He set about building a tower but at each attempt the foundations were found crumbling the following morning. Gwrtheyrn sought the advice of his magicians who told him to find a fatherless boy and have the earth around the foundations soaked with his blood.

A young lad named Myrddin Emrys was brought from South Wales but confounded the magicians with his wisdom. Myrddin (Merlin) stated that the reason for the failure to erect a tower was due to two fighting serpents in an underwater pool below. The boy's wisdom proved correct. After digging, a pool was discovered wherein were found sleeping a red dragon and a white dragon. Myrddin said that there would be no peace until the red dragon, which represented the Welsh, had fought off the white one, a symbol of the Saxons. The serpents fought, and the red one was eventually victorious.

A fortress was built, which Gwrtheyrn assigned to Myrddin, who on his departure left his treasure in a cave. Myrddin prophesised that one day a yellow haired youth with blue eyes would come to Dinas Emrys, step on a certain rock and that a bell would ring, opening an entrance to the cave. The blue eyed youth could then claim the treasure.

Archaeological evidence has revealed an artificial pool built to supply a settlement dating from the Iron Age. Occupation continued into the fifth century, a period generally associated with the legendary Gwrtheyrn and Myrddin. There are also the remains of a tower probably built by Llywelyn Fawr in the late twelfth century.

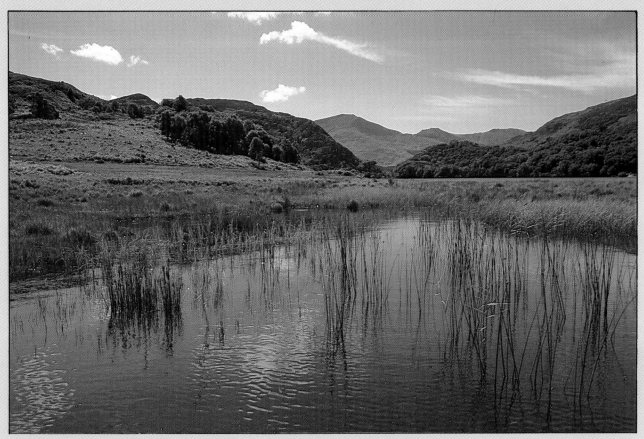

Dinas Emrys centre right across Llyn Dinas

25 SNOWDON (YR WYDDFA)

115 GR 610543

The old Welsh name for the rugged fastness containing Wales' highest peak was *Creigiau Eryri* (The Rocks of the Eagles). The golden eagle has long stopped breeding in North Wales and nowadays 'Eryri' is used to signify Snowdonia, a word derived from *Snawdun*, found in an early Saxon chronicle dating from 1095. *Snawdun* is believed to mean 'perpetually snow covered mountain', which Snowdon is not.

Giraldus, writing on the mountains of Eryri, mentions a tradition of an eagle that used to perch on a certain stone every fifth feast day to prey on the bodies of the slain, for sometime that day, war was expected. The stone had a hole in it formed by the bird constantly cleaning and sharpening its beak. This has given rise to the saying, 'The eagle knows the place, but not the time', while 'The raven knows the time, but not the place'. *Carreg yr Eryr* (The Rock of the Eagle) is mentioned as one of the bounds of Nant Gwynant in a charter granted by Llywelyn Fawr to the Abbey of Aberconwy.

In Welsh, Snowdon is known variously as *Yr Wyddfa Fawr* (The Great Tomb or The Great Throne) or *Carnedd y Cawr* (The Giant's Cairn) for its summit is the reputed grave of the giant Rhita, slain by Arthur. The mountain, with its surrounding peaks, ridges, *cymoedd* and lakes, is much celebrated in poetry and literature, and steeped in Arthurian legend.

Leaving Dinas Emrys, Arthur and his Knights headed for the upper reaches of Cwm Tregalan, where they confronted Mordred and his army. Arthur, leading, tried to force the enemy over into Cwm Dyli but fell in a shower of arrows at a spot known as *Carnedd Arthur* (Arthur's Cairn). The site of his last battle, the gap between Snowdon and the neighbouring peak of Lliwedd, is called *Bwlch y Saethau* (The Pass of the Arrows).

After his death, Arthur's Knights climbed the ridge of Lliwedd and descended to a cave below the crest called *Ogof Llanciau Eryri* (The Cave of Snowdonia's Youths). There the warriors remain, sleeping on their shields, awaiting the return of their hero to restore the crown of Britain to the *Cymry* (the Welsh). There is a Welsh saying:

> *'LLANCIA' 'RYRI A'U GWYN GYLL A'I HENNILL HI'*
> (SNOWDONIA'S YOUTHS WITH THEIR WHITE HAZELS WILL WIN IT)

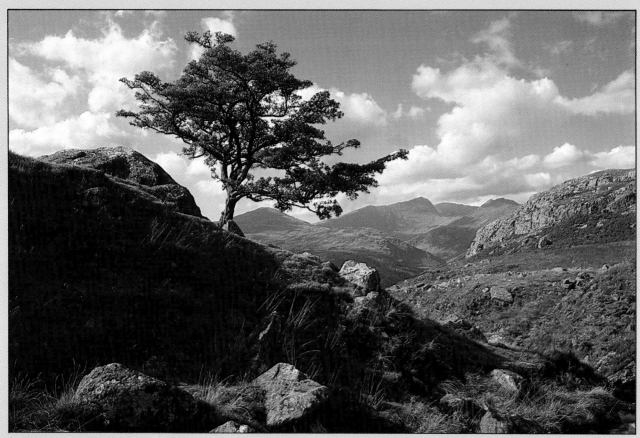

Snowdon from the slopes of Y Cnicht

26 GLASLYN

115 GR 615545

The deep bluish-green Glaslyn *(Blue Lake)* below Snowdon's precipices, at the head of Cwm Dyli, was originally called *Llyn y Ffynnon Las* (The Lake of the Green Well). Its unusual colour is a result of the extensive copper mining here in the eighteenth century. The sad ruins on the shore of Glaslyn, and the lower Llyn Llydaw, are reminders of man's past activities in this finest of Welsh *cymoedd*.

One of the highest lakes in Wales, there are several mysteries surrounding Glaslyn. It is said that nothing swims safely in it, hunted goats and deer having dived in and drowned. A fisherman was seen canoeing on its surface and shortly afterwards went mad and died. There is a tale of a young girl who emerged from its depths to wash clothes on the shore, and then returned to the lake. Glaslyn's most famous legend concerns the *afanc*, a mythical water monster, that was dragged there by Hu Gadarn and his team of oxen.

The *afanc* lived in a pool in Afon Conwy above Betws-y-coed and had caused great trouble by regularly flooding Dyffryn Conwy. A young girl was brought to entice it from the pool. The beast crawled out, and placing its huge scaly head on her lap, laid a claw on her breast. The giant Hu Gadarn lay in wait with chains, and his *Dau Ychan Bannog* (Two Long Horned Oxen). He bound the beast, which awoke in a rage, tearing the girl's breast off. The oxen dragged the thrashing monster towards Snowdon, through the gap above Llynnau Diwaunydd known as *Bwlch Rhiw'r Ychen* (the Pass of the Slope of the Oxen). Descending into Nant Gwynant, an ox lost an eye due to the strain, at a spot called *Gwaun Llygad Ych*, (the Marsh of the Ox Eye), a pool that never dries although no stream enters or flows from it.

Eventually Glaslyn was reached, wherein the mighty Hu dumped the *afanc*, where according to legend, it still remains.

Trioedd Ynys Prydain (the Welsh Triads), a list of legendary characters dating from the twelfth century, describes Hu Gadarn as a pacifist hero who first led the Welsh into Britain from the part of Asia that is known as Ceylon today. Hu introduced agriculture to the island and is credited with teaching the Welsh the art of ploughing.

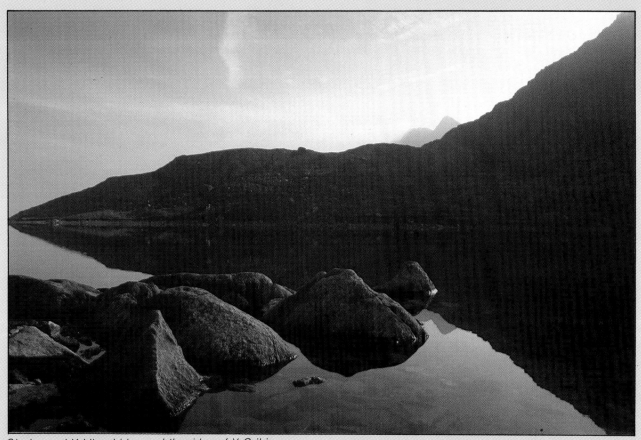

Glaslyn and Y Lliwedd beyond the ridge of Y Gribin

27 DYFFRYN MYMBYR

115 GR 715577

Llynnau Mymbyr lie below the northern slopes of Moel Siabod in the wide marshy valley between Capel Curig and Penygwryd.

The view of the Snowdon peaks from their shore is one of the most attractive in Wales. The origin of the word Mymbyr is obscure. Llyn Cwmffynnon above Pen y Pass was once known as Ffynnon Mymbyr and the stream flowing from it is known as Mymbyr. The Dyffryn neighbourhood has an unusual story of a fairy changeling. The fairies were often in the habit, usually on *Noswyl Ifan* (St. John's Eve) of exchanging their own deformed brats for the fair-headed unbaptized children of mortals.

One summer at the beginning of a poor harvest, the farmer's wife of Dyffryn Mymbyr gave birth to a fine, healthy boy. The weather being stormy and the farm some distance from a church, the parents neglected to baptize the child. One morning the mother went out to the field to work, leaving the baby in the care of its aged grandmother. The old woman fell asleep and the *Tylwyth Teg* crept into the house and stole the child, replacing it with a decrepit old man.

The grandmother awoke and in her anguish blew the horn to call the mother from the field. She rushed into the house and without looking at him clutched the cry-ing cretin to her breast. She sang a lullaby but nothing could calm him. On looking, and realizing it was not her son, she fell into a fit of despair. The husband was sent for and told to consult a *dyn hysbys* (soothsayer). Eventually, the parson of Trawsfynydd, who was skilled in the art of breaking spells, was contacted. The parson informed the father to take a shovel covered with salt and make the sign of the cross in it. He should then open the window of the room where lay the fairy child, and place the shovel on the fire until the salt burnt white hot. This the father did and the wretched changeling went away. In its stead the parents found their own boy unharmed on the doorstep.

There were several means of preventing the *Tylwyth Teg* from stealing a child: early baptism, the mother's presence, or tongs placed crossways on the cradle. Another way to reclaim a lost child was to have all the household folk hurl iron at the suspected changeling. This unpleasant act prompted the fairies to return the stolen child for they disliked any harm done to their own offspring. Superstition and fear of iron is a common theme in fairy folklore that may reflect a distant memory of a Bronze Age culture replaced by the succeeding Iron Age.

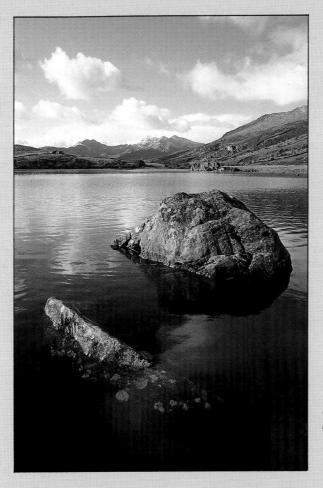

Snowdon Horseshoe from Llynnau Mymbyr

28 CASTELL DOLBADARN

115 GR 586598

The gaunt remains of this Welsh stronghold stand on a boomerang shaped outcrop overlooking Llyn Peris and Llyn Padarn. Geographically, the castle is a few metres outside the designated National Park boundary, but is included for its historic interest and grand setting.

Dolbadarn 'Padarn Meadow' may reflect a tradition with the sixth century saint, though the name is nowhere mentioned in any early bardic poetry or Welsh chronicles before 1200. *The Lives of the British Saints* (1907-13) states that 'at Llanberis—Padarn has his Nant, Llyn and Dôl. About two centuries ago the remains of a Capel Padarn were visible there at Llwyn Padarn in Dôl Badarn, on the lake side. But these may very well have derived their name from some other Padarn.'

Castell Dolbadarn's dominant feature is the circular keep, 14.6 metres high, which originally had a conical roof. It was built by Llywelyn Fawr in the early thirteenth century, in a key defensive position, guarding the northern end of the Llanberis pass. The castle controlled an ancient route through Snowdonia from Caernarfon to the upper Dyffryn Conwy. Dolbadarn later fell into the hands of Llywelyn's grandson, Llywelyn ap Gruffudd, the last Prince of Wales.

In 1255, after a battle for the rule of Gwynedd, Llywelyn ap Gruffudd defeated his brother Owain Goch (Owain the Red) and imprisoned him for over twenty years in the tower. After the second war of Welsh independence (1282-83) the castle was captured by Edward I who used its timber in the building of Caernarfon castle.

Dolbadarn was also where Owain Glyndŵr imprisoned his enemy, Lord Grey of Rhuthun, at the beginning of the uprising in the early fifteenth century.

In the eighteenth century Llanberis was a popular place for travellers and landscape painters in search of the 'grand', and the tower was a favourite pictorial subject. J.M.W.Turner, who was attracted to historic sites, sketched it during his visits in 1798 and 1799. His well known dramatic painting 'Dolbadarn Castle' was exhibited at, then later presented to, the Royal Academy of Arts. Dolbadarn is now in the care of Cadw, Welsh Historic Monuments.

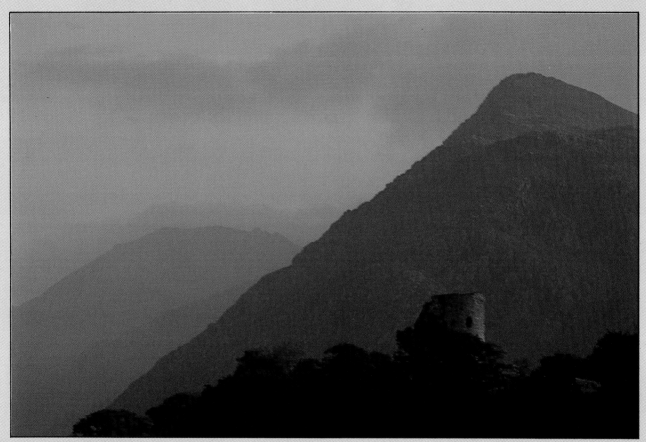

Llywelyn's Stronghold

29 CWM IDWAL

115 GR 645595

This is one of the most magnificent *cymoedd* in Britain, the first of fifteen National Nature Reserves established in Snowdonia. Only a short walk from one of the busiest roads in Wales, it is scientifically of great importance. The vast amphitheatre, hollowed out in the Ice Age, is a paradise for the student of geology and botany. The folding rocks of the headwall cliff, *Clogwyn y Geifr* (The Goats' Crag) is riven by the dark cleft called *Twll Du* (Devil's Kitchen). The moist, crumbling ledges hereabouts are the habitat of rare arctic and alpine flora. The Mountain Spiderwort *Lloydia Serotina* still survives and is found nowhere else in Britain outside Snowdonia.

The sweeping slabs and heathery walls at the far side of the lake are the playground of the climber. A hundred years ago, the damp gullies of Clogwyn y Geifr played an important part in the early history of Welsh climbing, producing appropriately named routes such as Hanging Garden Gully and Devil's Staircase.

The cirque lake in the floor of the *cwm* is quite shallow, being, for the most part, under four metres deep. Llyn Idwal owes its name in legend to a treacherous deed enacted on its shore.

Owain, a twelfth century Prince of Gwynedd, entrusted his youngest son Idwal to the care of his vain cousin, Nefydd Hardd. Nefydd was jealous of the scholarly Idwal, for his own son Dunawd was untalented. It was arranged for Dunawd to push Idwal into the lake wherein he drowned. Owain was informed and banished Nefydd from the Kingdom of Gwynedd, and named the lake Idwal in his son's memory.

Another tradition states that the land whereon stood the original Llanrwst church was given to Owain by Rhun ap Nefydd to compensate for his father's deed. It is said that no bird flies over the lake's surface, and that a wailing voice can be heard when there is a storm in the *cwm*.

The *cwm* is strewn with glaciated debris, and a moraine on the lake's western shore is reputed to be the burial place of Idwal, a giant. There is an excellent nature trail booklet on Cwm Idwal published by the Nature Conservancy Council.

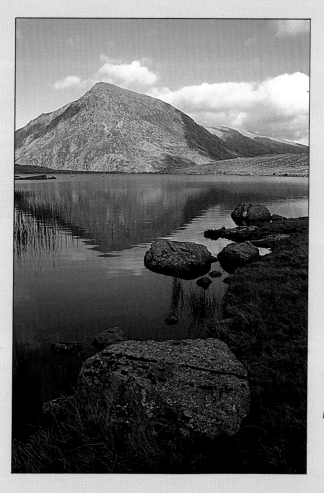

Llyn Idwal and Pen yr Ole Wen

30   MAEN Y BARDD (THE POET'S STONE)

115 GR 741718

Maen y Bardd cromlech is situated about a mile west of Ro-wen high above Dyffryn Conwy, beneath the ridge of Tal-y-fan in the northern Carneddau.

Cromlechs are the remains of the earliest surviving monuments of the Megalithic period. Their most distinguishing feature is a large capstone supported by three or four upright stones. They were erected as communal burial chambers between 2,000 and 4,000 BC by settlers entering Britain from the western seaways.

Maen y Bardd lies close to an ancient trackway which later became the Roman road from Caerhun to Caernarfon. Many such trackways criss-cross the landscape which must have been familiar to Neolithic man. Two miles north west of the cromlech on Penmaenmawr mountain is the Craig Lwyd axe factory, an important source of stone for the coastal trade in Neolithic stone axes.

The word 'cromlech' comes from the Welsh *crwm* (stooping) and *llech* (stone). North Wales is particularly rich in this type of monument and many are set in beautiful and remote areas that enhance the 'mystery of the past' that they evoke.

Several myths surround cromlechs. Many are associated with King Arthur hurling the huge stones from nearby summits, or angrily flinging irritating pebbles found in his shoe. Maen y Bardd is known locally as *Cwt y Bugail* (The Shepherd's Hut) and also *Cwt y Filiast* (The Greyhound Bitch's Kennel). Close by is a tall standing stone called *Ffon y Cawr* (The Giant's Stick) also known as Arthur's Spear. There is a legend concerning the cromlech and the stone which runs thus:

'A giant shepherd roamed the Carneddau hills, and one day while standing on Pen-y-gaer, he sent his dog up the ridge of Tal-y-fan to fetch some stray sheep. The dog, feeling idle, hid in the cromlech and fell asleep.

'On not being able to find his dog, the giant in his anger hurled his huge stick in the air. It struck the ground near the cromlech, shaking the capstone, which awoke the terrified greyhound, who from that day forth never disobeyed her master. The stick eventually turned to stone and remains to this day embedded in the same spot.'

At the northern end of the Glyder mountain group south of the Carneddau there is a peak called *Carnedd y Filiast* (The Greyhound Bitch's Cairn) perhaps a memorial to, or burial place of, the same greyhound. There is another peak of the same name north of Arennig Fawr. The female greyhound was one of the symbols of Ceridwen, goddess of poetry and inspiration.

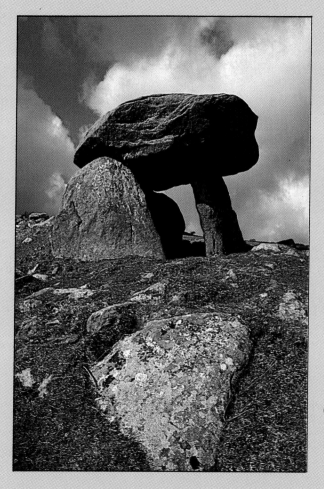

Cromlech of the Bard

31 LLANGELYNNIN OLD CHURCH

115 GR 751737

The old parish church of St. Celynnin stands 300 metres above sea level overlooking the lower Dyffryn Conwy. It is a lonely place, and its setting creates an atmosphere of conflict. As you stand above and look down on the windswept grey walls and church, there is a strong sense of the past, a presence of a very old Wales. Yet only a few miles below you can see the popular resorts of Conwy and Llandudno, bringing you back to the present. One can almost see the ghosts of the simple hillfolk toiling up the green slopes and passing along the churchyard wall on their way to prayer.

St. Celynnin was the son of Helyg Foel, and his descent can be traced back to Cunedda Wledig, a chieftain of Ystrad Clwyd, who drove the Irish out of Gwynedd. Cunedda's son Ceredig and grandson Meirion gave their names to the old counties of Ceredigion and Meirionnydd.

The medieval church originally consisted of a nave with a south porth, a chancel and north and south chapels. The south chapel was demolished in 1800. Inside is the remnant of a solid oak screen, very rare and found only in the earliest Celtic churches. On the east wall are some Welsh texts dating from 1600.

In the south west corner of the churchyard wall is the now roofless Ffynnon Gelynnin, a rectangular well paved with slabs. In the past, sick children were brought here and their clothing thrown into the water. If the clothing sank, the child was destined to die, but would live if they floated.

Fifty yards south of the well are the traces of a round hut with a clearly visible entrance. It may possibly be associated with an early Christian occupation. Those wishing to enter the church may obtain the key from the nearby farm of Garnedd-Wen.

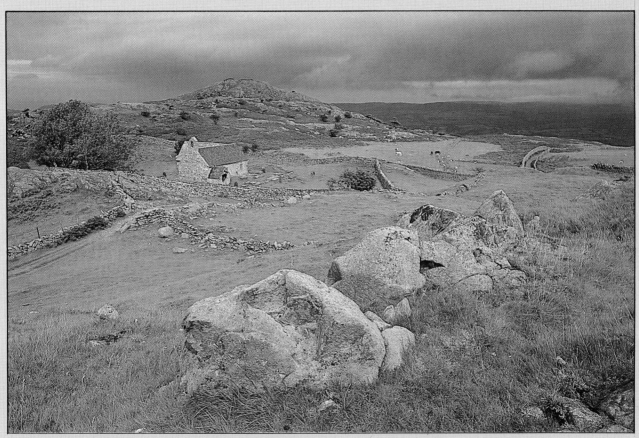

A strong sense of the past

32 EPILOGUE

It had been a good day. The hot hazy weather was over so I was glad of the first clear day. I went to Tomen y Mur in the morning then headed for Nanmor near Aberglaslyn. Some weeks earlier whilst camping at Beddgelert, I had taken my son Ceri up Y Cnicht from Nanmor. On our return we had followed the stream down from Llynnau Cerrig-y-myllt where the views of Snowdon are excellent. So, after returning to the slopes of Y Cnicht to photograph Snowdon I set off for home. Driving back towards Rhyd the setting sun looked splendid above Traeth Bach. I thought I would return to Tomen y Mur. Earlier in the morning at the fort a farmer had passed by several times, looking over the hedge, giving me suspicious looks. Perhaps he had thought I was a government official and that my tripod was some scientific apparatus?

I took a few shots of the fort and turning around there was a brilliant sunset over Llŷn. I was putting my camera away when, out of the shadows close by, came the farmer I had seen previously. He asked, in an abrupt manner, what was I doing. I told him politely that I was photographing the sunset. The farmer then became very friendly and asked if I would like to walk to the top of the hill to view the power station, which he quite rightly felt bitter about. He pointed out and knew the names of all the abandoned homesteads. Although having no education after primary school, or owning a television, he knew the history of his own beloved land.

We stood together in the dusk. Perhaps the weaver of the tale of Blodeuwedd had stood here? The Romans certainly had. The cromlech builders may have passed this way and their blood could be flowing in our veins. The farmer and I were strangers, yet fellow country-men, and here we were, silently watching the light fade over this fragile, ancient landscape.

CANMOL DY FRO A THRIG YNO
(PRAISE THY COUNTRY AND DWELL THERE)

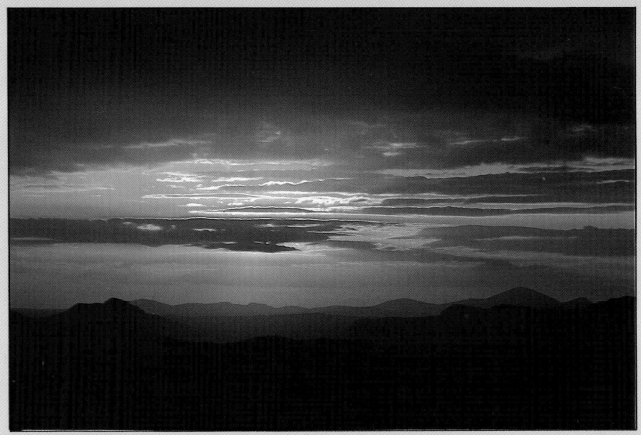

Sunset from Tomen y Mur

SHORT BIBLIOGRAPHY

All the research for this book was entirely my own, so I accept and apologise for any errors. There are many books on Snowdonia though unfortunatley the most interesting are now out of date and print. I would like to acknowledge the following list of authors and books which I have found most informative.

Avent, R. (1983) *Castles of the Princes of Gwynedd*
Barber, C. (1982) *Mysterious Wales*
Bowen, E.G. and Gresham, C.A. (1967) *History of Merioneth*
Cambrensis, G. (Everyman's Library 1908) *The Itinerary Through Wales*
Carr, H.R.C. and Lister, G.A. (1948) *The Mountains of Snowdonia*

Condry, W.M. (1966) *Snowdonia National Park*
Graves, R. (1961) *The White Goddess*
Jones G. and T. (1949) *The Mabinogion*
Jones, J. (1983) *The Lakes of North Wales*
North, F.T. Campbell, B. and Scott, R. (1949) *Snowdonia*
Owen, Rev. E. (1888) *Welsh Folklore*
Owen, H.J. (1950) *The Treasures of the Mawddach*
Pennant, T. (1784) *A Tour in Wales*
Rhys, J. (1901) *Celtic Folklore Welsh and Manx*
Royal Commission on Ancient Monuments (1956, 1960) *Caernarvonshire* Volume I and II
Stephens, M. (1986) Editor, *Oxford Companion to the Literature of Wales*
Ward, F. (1931) *The Lakes of Wales*

In the same series:

ARTISTS IN SNOWDONIA
James Bogle

A collection of thirty beautiful, atmospheric canvases by artists who, over the last two centuries, have tried to capture the grandeur of Wales' highest mountain range. Masterpieces by Turner are included alongside work by Welsh artists such as Richard Wilson, Augustus John and Kyffin Williams; with biographical notes and directions directing the reader to the exact spot where the pictures were painted. 88pp, A5 landscape format.

0 86243 222 7

We publish a wide range of books in Welsh and English. For a full list of publications, send now for our free, full-colour Catalogue – or simply surf into our Website!

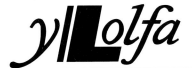

Talybont, Ceredigion, Cymru SY24 5AP
e-bost ylolfa@ylolfa.com
y we www.ylolfa.com
ffôn (01970) 832 304
ffacs 832 782
isdn 832 813